Nisbet Charles

The Usefulness and Importance of Human Learning

A Sermon Preached befroe the Trustees od Dickinson College

Nisbet Charles

The Usefulness and Importance of Human Learning
A Sermon Preached befroe the Trustees od Dickinson College

ISBN/EAN: 9783337156251

Printed in Europe, USA, Canada, Australia, Japan

Cover: Foto ©Lupo / pixelio.de

More available books at **www.hansebooks.com**

THE

USEFULNESS and IMPORTANCE

OF

HUMAN LEARNING,

S E R M O N

before the

TRUSTEES of DICKINSON COLLEGE.

Met at Carlisle, May 11, 1786; and publiſhed
at their Deſire.

By CHARLES NISBET, D. D. Principal of ſaid College.

" Doctrine ſed vi ... informat

" Rectique cultus pectora roborant."

HOR.

C A R L I S L E:

Printed by K L I N E & R E Y N O L D S.

At a Meeting of the BOARD of TRUSTEES of
DICKINSON COLLEGE, 11th May, 1786,

Refolved unanimoufly,

THAT the Thanks of this Board be prefented to the
Rev. Dr. NISBET, the Principal of this College,
for his Sermon delivered before the Truftees, Faculty and
Students this day; and that Mr. King and Mr. Smith be a
Committee to wait on the Doctor with this Addrefs of
Thanks, and to Requeft him to furnifh the Board with
a Copy in Order for Publication.

Extract from the Minutes,

THOMAS DUNCAN, Sec'y.

The USEFULNESS and IMPORTANCE
Of HUMAN LEARNING.

ACTS vii, 22. *And Moses was learned in all the Wisdom of the Egyptians, and was mighty in Words and Deeds.*

THE character, the history, the works and writings of Moses, occupy a distinguished place in the sacred volume. Remarkable from his birth for his wonderful preservation, and adoption by the daughter of the king of Egypt; afterwards for his sympathy and concern for his suffering brethren, and at last chosen of God to be their deliverer from slavery; we see united in his character the hero, the patriot and the legislator of a great people; the favorite of God, and the friend of men. In contemplating the lives of illustrious persons, we are apt to be dazzled with the splendor of their external actions, and ready to imagine that they must have been more than other men who performed them; while we do not attend to the secret causes and previous means by which they were prepared and enabled to

perform

(4)

perform them. But St. Stephen, in our text, reciting to his countrymen the hiſtory of Moſes, whom they highly reſpected, amidſt the ſingular honours and wonderful gifts conferred on him by his Creator, diſdains not to mention the human learning which he had received in the ſchools of Egypt, as one of thoſe means whereby he was prepared to act the diſtinguiſhed part to which he was deſtined by Divine Providence. Although God condeſcended to ſpeak with Moſes face to face, as a man ſpeaketh to his friend, altho' he was endowed with the ſpirit of prophecy and the gift of working miracles ; yet his human learning is mentioned by the inſpired martyr, as a neceſſary & notable ingredient in his exalted character. Moſes was born in a nation of ſlaves, whoſe minds were depreſſed by hard bondage ; and the low nature of thoſe labours which their cruel taſk-maſters impoſed on them, ſeems to have deſtroyed their courage, and rendered them unconſcious and inſenſible of the value of liberty, ſo that they were contented to continue ſlaves, with all their poſterity, provided only that they had the ordinary ſupports of life. If Moſes had been brought up in this manner ; if he had had only the low education and confined ideas of a ſlave, he could not have had any ſenſe of the value of liberty, nor conceive the leaſt notion of public
                                                       ſpirit ;

spirit; and consequently would have been an unfit instrument for instructing and delivering his countrymen. It is true that God might have inspired Moses with every kind of wisdom in an extraordinary manner, without the use of outward means; but altho' he can work miracles when he pleases, he never works them in vain, or in cases where ordinary means may serve the same purpose. It pleased God to rescue his chosen servant from the meanness of a slavish education, and to place him in such circumstances, that in a natural way, and by the use of common means, he might acquire a proper dignity of sentiment, the knowledge of men and things, a sense of the value of liberty, and of the necessity of regular government, and the various other accomplishments necessary for the legislator and conductor of a mighty people. And by this he has given a lesson to all ages, to teach us the usefulness of human learning; and how necessary it is that those should cultivate the powers of their mind who are destined to the important offices of government and legislation. For if Moses who was endowed with inspiration, stood in need of human learning for that purpose, it must be infinitely more necessary for us in these latter ages, when the gifts of prophecy and miracles are no longer indulged to men.

In

In difcourfing further on this fubject, it is propofed 1ft. more generally, to fhew the ufefulnefs of human learning. 2dly. to point out in particular its tendency to form good citizens, and to qualify youth for the moft eminent ftations in fociety, keeping in view the example of Mofes, and the benefits he derived from the wildom of the Egyptians; and in the laft place to make a few inferences from the doctrine delivered.

The firft thing propofed is to fhew the ufefulnefs of human learning in general.——And this may appear, 1ft; from that enlargement and ready exercife of the powers of the mind which it produces. No man is born learned, any more than he is born tall, ftrong or dexterous in the exercifes of the body. All our powers are at firft only weak, latent capacities, to be developed and improved by the courfe of time and application. The inftinct of nature, and the neceffities of life, excite us to the exercife of our bodily powers; but no more of our mental faculties are thereby excited, than fuch as are barely fufficient for the fupport and defence of the body: hence the rude form, and imperfect acquifitions of favage life, and the infant ftate of fociety and the ufeful arts among them. A favage may be endowed by nature with as large a portion of intellectual capacity as the moft accomplifhed

plifhed and lettered fage; but for the want of
exercife and occafions of excitement, it lan-
guifhes in obfcurity, and inaction, and re-
mains equally unknown and ufelefs to himfelf and others.

Education, by calling the mind into exercife,
difcovers its formerly unknown powers, and
excites its dormant capacities to lively action.
Hence habits of thinking are produced, and
the foul, now confcious of its powers, is
led to exercife them on a great variety of
objects; the field of imagination and reflection is vaftly enlarged, and the mind profits
the more by its new acquifitions, that the
faculty of thinking is capable of inceffant
exercife. The powers of the body, being
weak and limited, cannot be excited beyond
a certain degree, otherwife wearinefs, difeafe and death muft be the confequence;
but the powers of the mind are of an unknown range and compafs: inftead of being wearied, they acquire vigor and in-
creafe by proper excitement and exercife,
and are capable of infinitely greater improvement and variety than thofe of the body. The power of thinking, like all others,
becomes ftronger by exercife; and as in me-
chanics, it is experience, practice and application that lead to improvement and excellence, fo in thinking, thofe who have been
moft employed in ftudy, and the exercife of
their

their mental powers, muſt neceſſarily be more expert, ingenious and diſcerning than others. The human faculties, when confined within too narrow a ſphere, as muſt be the caſe when not excited and enlarged by education, find no opportunity of exertion, and languiſh for want of exerciſe, ſo that they remain uſeleſs to the poſſeſſor and to the public: but learning and philoſophy, by leading the mind to reflection, make it acquainted with itſelf and its own powers, with its nature, ſituation, dignity and intereſt, as well as with the nature of ſurrounding objects, their relation to man, and their fitneſs for exciting his capacities and promoting his happineſs. And how uſeful theſe acquiſitions are for the conduct, improvement and embelliſhment of human life, we need not ſpend time to prove.

2d. The uſefulneſs of human learning will further appear, if we conſider that inſatiable and ſtrong deſire of knowledge which is implanted in the human mind by its great Creator. God has been pleaſed to furniſh every creature with thoſe inſtincts and propenſities which he knew to be uſeful for promoting their happineſs, and from his having given this deſire of knowledge in ſo great a degree to men, we may fairly infer its uſefulneſs. God does nothing in vain. He has made knowledge agreeable to the

human

human foul, as light is to the eye of the body. Knowledge is the food and the delight
of the mind; and altho' that defire or curi-
ofity which leads to the acquifition of knowledge is at firft dormant, and fcarcely dif-
cernible; although in many it is ftifled by
other more powerful propenfities, and like a
mufical ear, muft be excited by external caufes
circumftances; yet when once properly ex-
& cited, it gradually gathers ftrength, and becomes a powerful principle of action. The
purfuit of knowledge itfelf, independent of
the ufefulnefs and excellence of thofe objects
with which it makes us acquainted, forms
an agreeable and enchanting exercife to the
human faculties, which to fome has fuch
charms, as to lead them to relinquifh all
other purfuits on this account. Through
defire, fays Solomon, a man having fepa-
rated himfelf, feeketh and intermeddleth
with all wifdom. Thus the love of knowledge often becomes a counterpoife to the
love of vice; and amidft the temptations of
an evil world, affords an occupation to the
human faculties, at once fuitable to their
dignity, and tending to their improvement.

3dly. The ufefulnefs of human learning
may appear from the help it affords to mo-
rais. Philofophy is never more properly and
worthily employed, than when it is applied
to the difcovery of our moral nature, and

B   the

the great end of our creation; and the
knowledge which it affords us of the dignity
of the human foul, our relation to the Deity, and our duty refulting from that relation, may be confidered as luminous proofs
of its ufefulnefs and excellence. To the
crude thoughts of fimple and unlettered
men, mankind appear as fo many loofe, independent & unconnected individuals, having each a feparate intereft, and naturally dif-
pofed to make war with one another. Such
inaccurate views tend to nourifh a felfifh fpirit, a neglect of the duties of fociety, & a to-
tal indifference for the public. But philofophy
leads our thoughts to a common origin and
brotherhood, explains the nature & progrefs
of fociety, and the advantages of affociation
and concord among men, the facred relation
conftituted by marriage, the charities of kin-
dred, the relation and duties of parents and
children, the fweets of friendfhip, the benefits
of peace, and the ftrength & fecurity which
every individual derives from the protection
of fociety. It likewife difclofes to us the
mifchiefs of difcord & the indulgence of the
unfocial paffions, that benevolence which we
owe to all who partake of the fame nature
with ourfelves, the excellence and neceffity
of the virtues of juftice, meeknefs, compaf-
fion and focial affection, which form the ce-
ment of all well-ordered communities of
men,

men. Thus the very subjects with which
philosophy is chiefly conversant, are so many proofs of its usefulness, and its tendency
to improve the human character, and to promote the happiness of mankind.

4thly. The usefulness of human learning
will further appear from its bringing us acquainted with many illustrious and exempla-
ry characters, and putting us in possession
of the collected wisdom and experience of
past ages. The short term and limited situ-
ation of human life, confines the wisdom
and experience of each individual within
very narrow bounds. Few are so situated
as to be acquainted with many illustrious
characters, or to have an opportunity of acquiring worthy sentiments or useful knowledge from their acquaintance ; besides that
the greatest part of human life is past in those
common and ordinary actions, which scarce-
ly distinguish one man from another. But
while philosophy unveils the principles, nature and tendency of human actions, history
draws back the curtain that conceals the
great theatre of the world, and discloses to
us in their due succession and proper dimen-
sions the illustrious dead of all former ages,
makes us acquainted with their characters,
manners, situations and transactions, their
wisdom, their virtues and their weaknesses,
so that the astonished student becomes as it
were

were cotemporary with all ages, a citizen of all countries, and perfonally acquainted with the moft diftinguifhed of the human fpecies: he fees empires rife and fall before him; he difcerns the moft important events in their fprings and caufes; he fees arts fometimes encouraged and protected, fometimes extinguifhed and fwept away by returning barbarity; he traces the origin of fcience and of the various forms of government; he difcerns thofe virtues that conftitute and preferve the happinefs of fociety; and thofe vices which always tend to, and often produce its diffolution; and with a fhorter experience of the miferies of human life, he acquires as much wifdom as probably he would have acquired, had he lived from the beginning of the world to the prefent time. The power of example in forming and affimilating the characters of men, is univerfally acknowledged to be fuperior to that of precept; and the man who fees nothing to admire and imitate in the illuftrious examples and accumulated wifdom of paft ages recorded in hiftory, muft either be very proud, or very dull. In fociety it is ordinary for men to refemble the company they keep, and the characters which they approve. "He that walketh with wife men, fhall be wife, but a companion of fools fhall be deftroyed." And although human hiftory

tory

tory confifts, in a great meafure, in a relation of the vices and follies of men ; yet in
every age we may find fome worthy and exalted characters, whofe virtues are rendered
more illuftrious by the corruption of the times
wherein they lived. It is certainly fit & ufeful
that youth fhould be made acquainted with
thefe examples, from the imitation of which
they may derive fignal profit; nor will the
knowledge of vicious characters be wholly
ufelefs to them : they may learn to defpife
their bafenefs, now no longer concealed by
the fplendor of their condition, and to take
warning from their errors, when they confider the deferved infamy with which moft
of their characters are covered, and tranf-
mitted to pofterity. The characters of the
living are commonly obfcured by flander
and envy, or leffened by fome of thofe weak-
neffes that are infeparable from human nature, fo that whatever excellence they may
pollefs, they are always feen to difadvant-
age : but envy has nothing to do with the
dead, and time conceals their weaknefs, fo
that they appear in a more favourable and
engaging light than if we were perfectly
acquainted with them.

5thly. Human learning is ufeful, on account of its fubferviency to religion. The
divine attributes are made manifeft by the
works of nature, which it is the bufinefs of
philofophy

philofophy to furvey, and the knowledge it
affords us of the greatnefs and immenfity of
the univerfe, and of the inconceivable wifdom, power and goodnefs difplayed in its
formation and prefervation, while they fi-
lence the Atheift, they lead the devout to
juft notions of their own dependant ftate,
and reverent apprehenfions of the great ob-
ject of all adoration. Perhaps the moft beneficial difcovery afforded us by philofophy,
is that of its own weaknefs and infuffici-
ency; but a flight acquaintance with it
will not lead to this difcovery. Philofophy knows nothing of creation or the beginning of things ; is often at a lofs to re-
concile the events of Providence to the attributes of the Deity, and is utterly unable to
inform us how our evil paffions may be con-
quered, how a juft God can pardon finners,
or how thefe can be made good who are
accuftomed to do evil. It is true that philofophy offers prefcriptions for removing
our moral diforders ; but alas! experience
difcovers their futility and want of efficacy.
To contemplate the beauty of virtue and
the deformity of vice, to meditate on the
dignity of human nature, and to ftruggle
againft our natural inclinations, are weak & in-
effectual remedies for creatures under the influence of corrupt nature, paffion and ha-
bit, and confequently incapable of ufing thefe
remedies

remedies properly, if they were of any real utility. The doubts and darkness into which philosophy leads us in many subjects, afford us useful lessons of humility, and dispose us to receive with gratitude the light of divine revelation. The man who imagines that every thing is discoverable and resolvable by reason, is not sufficiently acquainted with its powers and extent. " A little learning is a dangerous thing" In the present age there is a general diffusion and communication of knowledge, in some degree, to every rank in civilized countries ; but as real learning can not be acquired without pain and application, the far greater part content themselves with a little smattering of it, and a few general indigested notions, of which they are exceedingly proud, and fond of displaying their little stores. Hence we ought to trace the progress of pert and disputatious infidelity, which is so rampant in the present age. It is probable that there are but few systematic and determined Infidels, who having examined with some attention the proofs of Christianity, think them insufficient to command their assent. The most of our modern Infidels are made without study or meditation of any kind, and generally have very little reading, except perhaps a few scraps from Voltaire, or some other of the patriarchs of infidelity. But almost all of them

are

are totally unacquainted with the Christian
system, which they pretend to confute, as
well as with that philosophy which they ignorantly imagine to be on their side. By the
help of a few cant words, such as priest-
craft, superstition, credulity, right reason
and true philosophy, which they have either borrowed from books or received by
tradition, accompanied by a great deal of
oaths, and such ribaldry and effrontery as
sound philosophy disdains, they impudent-
ly impose their foolish opinions upon the
young and inattentive, while they laugh at
all who believe any others except themselves.
Many young and untaught persons, by keeping bad company, and addicting themselves
to fashionable vices, endeavour to defend
their conduct, and to silence the reproaches
of their conscience by assuming the profession of infidelity, though ignorant of the arguments it usually adopts: some make the
same profession from the love of singularity,
or in order to appear wiser than others,
whence we often find the sacred truths of
Christianity ridiculed by men who know not
what they say, nor whereof they affirm,
while they assume the air of profound philosophers, and boast of having overcome
the prejudices of their education. Stupifi-
ed by the amusements of a thoughtless life,
and puffed up by the praises of those who
know

know as little as themselves, they presume
to decide the most abstruse and difficult
questions in the midst of riot and intemper-,
ance ; they think they are possessed of true
wisdom, and look down with contempt,
from their imaginary height, upon the
thoughtful and religious part of mankind.
While such odious and futile characters
abound, nothing can be more necessary for
youth than the study of true philosophy,
which will effectually guard them against being seduced by these superficial talkers, and
enable them to encounter the enemies of religion, on that ground which they so much
vaunt, and with which they think they are
acquainted; and to convince them, if they are
willing to be convinced, that philosophy can
not resolve every difficulty, nor remove all
the evils of our nature ; and that the Christian faith which they ignorantly despise, has
not only miracles and prophecies, but reason and argument on its side.

The second thing we proposed was to
point out in particular the necessity and usefulness of human learning to societies, and
its tendency to form good citizens, from the
example of Moses, and the benefit he derived from the wisdom of the Egyptians.---
Indeed every thing we have said already may
be considered as an argument in favour of
this assertion, as wise and well instructed in-

C   dividuals

dividuals compofe the greateft ftrength of the ftates to which they belong, and from having cultivated their minds and enlarged their experience by ftudy, are incomparably the beft qualified for the intricate bufinefs of government and legiflation, if their countrymen are wife enough to call them into office. Without wife and virtuous men in the offices of adminiftration, no ftate can preferve its reputation abroad, nor its order, profperity and exiftence at home. Men of weak underftandings and confined ideas can neither uniformly difcover, nor fteadily attend to the public intereft. Wrapt up in their own concerns, deftitute of experience, and fond of their " little brief authority," they cannot be expected to have proper notions of honour and juftice, or of the fanctity of public and private faith, and may fometimes by a ftretch of power enact laws to ftop the courfe of juftice, to encroach on the rights of property, and to render the public faith uncertain and infignificant, while their numbers render them incapable of blufhing for the iniquity they have eftablifhed by law.---Nothing can be more pernicious and difgraceful to a ftate, than fuch men and fuch meafures. And here I cannot forbear mentioning with the moft fincere approbation, the feventh article of the conftitution of this ftate, by which it is provided that " the house

house of representatives of the freemen of
this commonwealth, shall confist of persons
most noted for wisdom and virtue." If this
article of the constitution is strictly adhered
to, we need not be apprehensive that any
such disorders will ever take place in this
state. But, to proceed.

Moses was destined by Providence to be
a ruler and a judge to God's chosen people ;
and the more that his faculties were exer-
cised, and his ideas and experience enlarged
by study, he would be better acquainted
with human nature, and more fit for his exalted station, and for bearing, directing and
governing the humours and passions of men,
while he led them invariably to their true
interest. And it appears that God designed
that he should have these advantages, by
placing him in a station where he had the
best opportunities which the world then afforded for acquiring them.

It is difficult indeed, at this distance of
time, to give a particular account of the
Egyptian learning in which Moses was instructed ; one circumstance especially contri-
butes to increase this difficulty. The Egyptians, though a learned, yet were not a lettered nation ; and in the time of Moses were
utter strangers to alphabetical writing. Their
learning therefore must have been merely
traditionary, and preserved only in the me-
mories

mories of their priests, like that of the Druids of ancient Gaul and Britain. Letters were not invented early enough to preserve the Egyptian learning, so that the original monuments of it are lost many ages ago. Besides, perhaps to conceal the scantiness of their stores, they affected to make a great mystery of their learning, communicating it only to particular persons, with great chariness and circumspection. Had not Moses been in favour at court, as the adopted son of Pharaoh's daughter, he would not have been initiated in the misteries of Egyptian wisdom. In a later age a Greek philosopher, travelling into Egypt, needed the recommendation of a sovereign prince, in order to be admitted to this privilege.

On these accounts we should at this day have been wholly ignorant of the learning of ancient Egypt, were it not from the hints thrown out in the sacred history, and the diligence and curiosity of a few Greeks, particularly Plato, Iamblichus, Diodorus Siculus and Philo Byblius whose fragments have been preserved by Eusebius. Some tracts of Plutarch have likewise preserved a few traditions.

From these we learn that Egypt was the native country of geometry and mathematics, which the particular circumstances of that country rendered very necessary. It was the
principal

principal mart of knowledge reforted to by
the oldeft of the Greek philofophers, before
their vanity had perfuaded them that they
could invent every thing of themfelves, and
Thales one of the feven fages, brought from
Egypt the firft fun dial that was feen in Europe; from which circumftance, and their
accurate computation of the length of the
year, it appears that they were not ignorant
of the principles of aftronomy; nay Pythagoras is faid to have learned in Egypt what
is is now called the Copernican fyftem.

That natural philofophy was well underftood among them is evident from the flourifhing ftate of the mechanic arts, which is
evinced by monuments ftill extant. The
conftruction of their pyramids, temples and
obelifks, with fome fpecimens of ancient
painting and gilding yet to be feen in that
country, but efpecially their art of embalming dead bodies fo as to preferve them incorrupted for the fpace of three thoufand years,
are fignal proofs of this fact, and the wonderful works of their magicians or jugglers,
related in facred hiftory, prove that they
were poffeffed of fecrets which have not defcended to fucceeding ages. It is likewife
probable that Bezaleel and Aholiab, whofe
ingenuity adorned the tabernacle of God,
tho' it is faid that they were filled with wifdom by the fpirit of God, learned the firft
rudiments of their fkill under Egyptian artifts.

Their embalming led them to some knowledge of anatomy and phyfic ; and we are told that they had particular phyficians for every difeafe known among them'; nor were they ignorant of the philofophy of the mind, being among the firft who afferted the immortality of the foul, and a future ftate of rewards and punifhments, of which doctrine they made great ufe in their civil policy.

It is eafy to fhow that thefe fciences into which Mofes was initiated in Egypt muft have greatly contributed to elevate, exercife and enlarge his mind ; but what particularly diftinguifhed the antient Egyptians ; and from which perhaps Mofes profited more than from all the reft, was their arts of government and legiflation ; and although under this head the moft of their inftitutions are totally unknown, yet the certain effects of them narrated in hiftory, are truly aftonifhing. The orderly form of fociety among them, the improvement of the arts, the exactnefs of their police, the riches of their country, the fecurity of life and property, and the ready obedience and happinefs of the people, are fo many fignal proofs of the excellence of their political inftitutions, and accordingly attracted the admiration of other nations, even after they were not a little degenerated from their antient cuftoms.

cuftoms. Perhaps it was chiefly in the article of policy and civil wifdom that Mofes was indebted to the Egyptian learning, as though he received his laws immediately from the Deity, yet in his ordinary behaviour as a ruler, and in the promulgation, execution and application of them, he was left to the dictates of political prudence and experience. Although the Egyptians had flaves whom they treated with rigor, as all mafters of flaves do more or lefs, yet the natives were governed by fixed laws, which guarded their lives and properties, and even humanifed the unrelenting fpirit of monarchy. When Mofes had flain an Egyptian, though he was in high favour at court, he was obliged to abandon Egypt, having reafon to dread the wrath of the king and the vengeance of the laws, which he would have had no reafon to dread, had he lived under fome modern princes and ftates. The government of Egypt indeed was monarchial, but their laws appear to have been wife and impartial, and the priefts who poffeffed the power of judicature, feem to have contributed to balance the royal authority in favour of public juftice and the private happinefs of the fubjects. Moreover, being poffeffed of independent fortunes, and monopolifing almoft all the learning of their times, it appears that they were greatly refpected

both

both by the fovereign and the people; fo that
Jofeph, a minifter introduced and appoint-
ed by the crown, was obliged to ally himfelf to the priefthood, in order to render
his adminiftration more refpectable and a-
greeable to the people.

So habituated were the Egyptians to order and regularity, and fo much were they
convinced of the benefits of peace and concord, that when Jacob and his family were
brought into the land of Gofhen, till then
unoccupied, we do not find that it excited
the leaft murmur or jealoufy among the
natives, nor that any of them pretended to
have prior grants to the lands occupied by
the houfe of Ifrael. And in the time of feven
years of famine, we read not of the leaft tu-
mult or diforder on that account; though
under the boafted policy of Rome, both in
the times of the republic and the emperors,
we read of frequent diforders on occafion
of fcarcity, though for much fhorter periods. Nay when Jofeph had bought the
whole land for Pharaoh, and, in order to ef-
tablifh a fettled revenue, had granted it back
to the fubjects on new terms; when he
tranfported the natives from the one end of
the kingdom to the other, they patiently
fubmitted, from a regard to juftice, and a
conviction of the validity of the refignation
they had made of their lands into the hands
of

of the king, in return for his supporting them during the famine.

It is true that this degree of obedience may be thought flavish, but it proves that they had been long habituated to order, and convinced of the benefits of regular government, else they would not have carried their obedience on this occasion, to an excess. God, in ordering the affairs of the world, has shewn more regard to the order and general peace of society, and the preservation of justice, than to the liberty of states and individuals. Liberty is a blessing which has always been bestowed with a sparing hand and for short periods, on the children of men; and no wonder, because it requires wisdom, a gift still more rare, to manage it to advantage. Those who are favoured with this precious gift, ought certainly to shew their thankfulness to God for it, by a humble, just, regular and religious life, and to ask of him that wisdom which is necessary to render their liberty a blessing, and particularly to chuse such men to the offices of government as possess a sense of honour and a love of justice, who know the use, as well as the value of liberty, and who consider the interest of the state as inseparably connected with public faith, the sacred obligation of contracts, and the rights of property. But to return, Moses being well ac-

D   acquainted

quainted with human nature, and initiated
in the political wifdom of Egypt, was therefore a proper perfon to manage a large fociety, and to lead them to their duty by con-
vincing them that it was their intereft.
Hence he is faid to have been mighty in
words and in deeds, by which it is not meant
that he was an artificial rhetorician, as we
are affured that he was deftitute of a grace-
ful pronunciation, which is one of the principal charms of that art. But he was a rati-
onal and wife philofopher, who had learned
to think with propriety, perfpicuity and
dignity, and to fupport his arguments with
the ftrength of reafon. Words are only the
copies of the thoughts, made fenfible to the
ear, and by that means conveyed to the
minds of others. Although the grandeur and
propriety of the thoughts of Mofes excited
the admiration even of heathen criticks, he
never affected the artificial ornaments of
rhetoric. Even his poetry is beautifully fimple, though truly fublime. Mofes was not
a noify and fuperficial talker, without knowledge of bufinefs or capacity for action, but
he had learned to act as well as to fpeak with
propriety, without which his fpeeches would
have been of fmall advantage to his character,
or to the public. The Grecian hero in
Homer gives us a brief defcription of a good
education, when he tells us that his tutor
taught

taught him to imitate the best examples, to study to excel others, to be a speaker of speeches and a doer of deeds. To think, to speak and act with propriety and dignity, comprises all the wisdom of which man is capable; and this we are assured that Moses learned in part from the wisdom of the Egyptians. And even the disciples of our blessed Saviour, the perfection of whose nature rendered instruction superfluous to him, in describing his character, could say nothing more honourable of him than that he was a prophet mighty in deed and word, before God and all the people. The acquired wisdom of Moses was profitable to the public, as well as honourable to himself: he thought, spoke and acted for the welfare of men, and the benefits which his countrymen derived from his administration are so many proofs how useful human learning is to society, and how much it is for the interest of states to have their legislators and rulers properly instructed and qualified for their offices as he was. We shall conclude with a few inferences.

1st. From what has been said we ought to learn not to despise human learning as if it were an useless and idle amusement, & of no importance to society. The contrary, we think, has been made abundantly evident from the example before us. Some smatterers,

terers, truants from fchool, or imperfectly
inftructed, affect to treat it as entirely ufelefs;
but no man who has a tolerable acquaintance
with it can think meanly of its importance.
It is with a bad grace that the ignorant rail
againft what they do not underftand. Wifdom is juftified of her children, and thofe
who have not been converfant with it, have
no right to pronounce any judgment con-
cerning it. It is true that learning can not
work miracles, and that there have been
learned men of trifling, ridiculous, and even
abominable characters, but this is not owing
to their learning, but to the original wicked-
nefs and vices of their mind, which no philofophy can entirely fubdue.

2d. From what has been faid we may fee
the tendency of learning to make good citizens. and the obligation that all ftates are
under, to fupport and promote it. Some
will fay that they deftine their children for
humble and ordinary ftations, fuch as learning is not thought neceffary to adorn: but
in a popular government who can fay what
perfons may or may not be chofen members
of the legiflature, and entrufted with the
interefts of the public? And how unfortu-
nate muft that ftate be, that is governed by
ignorant, mean and felfifh men! In a republic the advantages of learning ought to
be diffufed as far as poffible, that wherever
the

the public choice may light, there may be some probability that the person chosen, may be in some measure qualified for public trust. We mean not to derogate from the merit of plain sense and unlettered wisdom; but though some, by the goodness of nature, and the improvement of intelligent company, or private study, may have been beneficial to the public, without the advantage of human learning, yet such instances are rare, and such persons would have been still more useful if they had been learned: besides, persons of this sort are never enemies to learning, but commonly its greatest friends and admirers. Learning is certainly the surest and most direct way of being prepared for doing the duties of good citizens, and especially for the offices of government and legislation, for discharging which knowledge and experience are essentially requisite.

3dly. From what has been said, let us learn not to overvalue human learning, or to imagine that it is sufficient to lead us to true felicity. Learning carries us a little way, with much pleasure, and tolerable evidence, it leads to great advantages, and preserves from many errors, but it falls short of leading us to eternal happiness. This is the office of revealed religion, which will be valued by every man who possesses true learning.

Socrates,

Socrates, with whom none of our modern
infidels, are worthy to be named, spoke of
divine revelation with reverence, and sup-
posing it indulged to man, declared that it
ought to be received with gratitude and ve-
neration. But our minute philosophers,
without having studied human nature, or
read the bible with attention, treat the doc-
trines of revelation, which they have never
examined, with a disdainful smile. The
man who is proud of his knowledge, evi-
dently shews that he has got little to be proud
of. A little knowledge puffeth up, but true
learning and philosophy which teach us to
contemplate God in his works, lead its pos-
sessors to humility and devotion. When the
Psalmist had considered the heavens, the
work of God's fingers, the moon and the
stars that he had ordained, he cried out,
" Lord, what is man, that thou art mindful
" of him, or the son of man, that thou vi-
" sitest him!

4thly. From what has been said let the
youth of this seminary be excited to diligence
and application to the study of learning, and
for this purpose, to think justly of its dignity, its usefulness, and its tendency to make
good citizens. Perhaps some of you may
not yet be duly apprised of the importance
of your present studies, and their influence
on your future usefulness and welfare, but
in

in proportion as you advance in learning, and
your knowledge of things is enlarged, you
will be more fenfible of the advantages of a
liberal education, and of its tendency to
qualify you for every ftation to which your
country may call you. And although in the
prefent courfe of things " the race is not to
" the fwift, nor the battle to the ftrong, nor
" favour to men of fkill, nor bread to the
" wife, nor riches to men of underftanding;
" but time and chance happeneth to all," yet
we may affure you that you will never have
caufe to repent of your application to your
ftudies; and if you fhould not be called to
places of truft and importance, you will have
the confolation to think, and perhaps to convince others, that you have deferved them.
Learning is no lefs fit to adminifter confolation, and to afford refources to the mind in
adverfity, than to adorn profperity. Cultivate the powers of your minds, and apply
yourfelves to the knowledge of men and
things, as if you knew for certain that the
moft diftinguifhed ftations and places in the
ftate were referved for you. Remember
that in every kind of bufinefs it is the hand
of the diligent that maketh rich. Your being well educated will be fo far from hin-
dering your advancement in the world, that
if your countrymen are wife, it will mark
you out for their choice, and qualify you to
discharge

difcharge the truft repofed in you, with
honour and advantage. Confider that on
your prefent behaviour your future confe-
fequence and ufefulnefs neceffarily depend.
If Mofes needed diligent application to various ftudies, and it appears by his ready cal-
cination of the golden calf, that he had not
neglected any part of them, though he had
the gift of prophecy and working miracles ;
diligence muft be much more neceffary for
you, ~~who have no reafon to expect~~ fuperna-
~~tural gifts.~~ Your parent ~~reqed that~~ you
will be diligent, and much of their happinefs depends on your fuccefs and good conduct. " A wife fon maketh a glad father,
" but a foolifh fon is the heavinefs of his
" mother." May God Almighty incline
your minds to the love and ftudy of true
wifdom, and turn all our labours to your
~~benefit and that the publ~~ that you may
be qualified to fulfil and adorn every ftation,
and may, like Mofes, be mighty in words
and in deeds.

F I N I S.

www.ingramcontent.com/pod-product-compliance
Lightning Source LLC
Chambersburg PA
CBHW021458090426
42739CB00009B/1774